THAT'S OUR PRINCIPAL!

The author wishes to thank everyone at P.S. 87, Manhattan, for their generosity, support, and inspiration in the making of this book.

Text © 2003 by Ann Morris
Photographs and illustrations © 2003 by Peter Linenthal

Library of Congress Cataloging-in-Publication Data

Morris, Ann, 1930-
That's our principal!/Ann Morris ; photographs and illustrations by Peter Linenthal.
p. cm.—(That's our school)
Summary: Introduces Steve Plaut, an elementary school principal, describing what he does during the school day and how he interacts with other staff and students.
ISBN 0-7613-2374-0 (lib. bdg.)
1. Elementary school principals—Juvenile literature. [1. School principals. 2. Occupations.] I. Linenthal, Peter, ill. II. Title.
LB2831.9.M67   2003
372.12'012—dc21   2002152487

The Millbrook Press, Inc.
2 Old New Milford Road
Brookfield, Connecticut 06804
www.millbrookpress.com

THAT'S OUR PRINCIPAL!

Ann Morris

Photographs and Illustrations
by Peter Linenthal

The Millbrook Press / Brookfield, Connecticut

We have a
great principal.
His name is
Steve Plaut.

He is very busy and comes to school early each morning.

At our school you can find him everywhere . . .

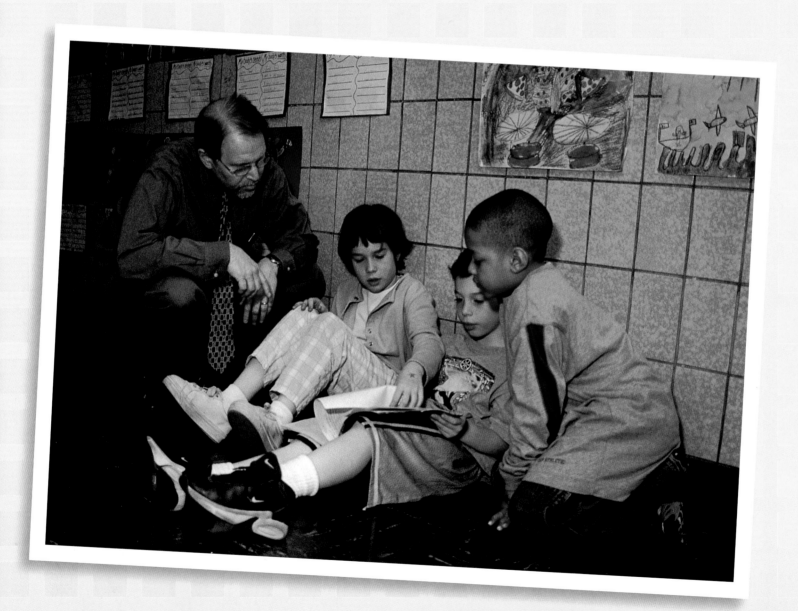

talking with students,
finding out what they are
reading, writing, and thinking,
saying good-bye when they leave.

Our principal is
in charge of everything . . .
the building, the school
workers, the students.
He helps make sure
the school is a good
place to learn.
In the morning he
meets with his secretary
and assistant principal.
They help him
plan the day.

Our principal meets often with school workers to make sure that everything works. Sometimes he goes over safety rules with the school guard.

Our principal talks to a lot of people on the phone. He orders supplies for the school. He calls parents about school business.

Our principal often meets with teachers and parents.
They talk about what the children need to help them learn.
Sometimes he helps plan assemblies and other school activities.

On some days our
principal is so busy
he eats lunch at his desk.
But we know we
can always visit
him in his office.
We can talk with him
about our work and
about how we feel.

Our principal likes to visit us in our classroom.

"What are you doing?" he asks during our

arithmetic lesson.

Sometimes he helps us with our work.

Sometimes he talks with
us in the lunchroom.

Or he stops by the
library to share a joke.

During Reading
Week our principal
dressed up as
Captain Hook,
the pirate.
That was funny!

One day he read stories to us.

Mr. Plaut is always friendly and interested in what we're doing.

But there are times when he has to remind children of the school rules.

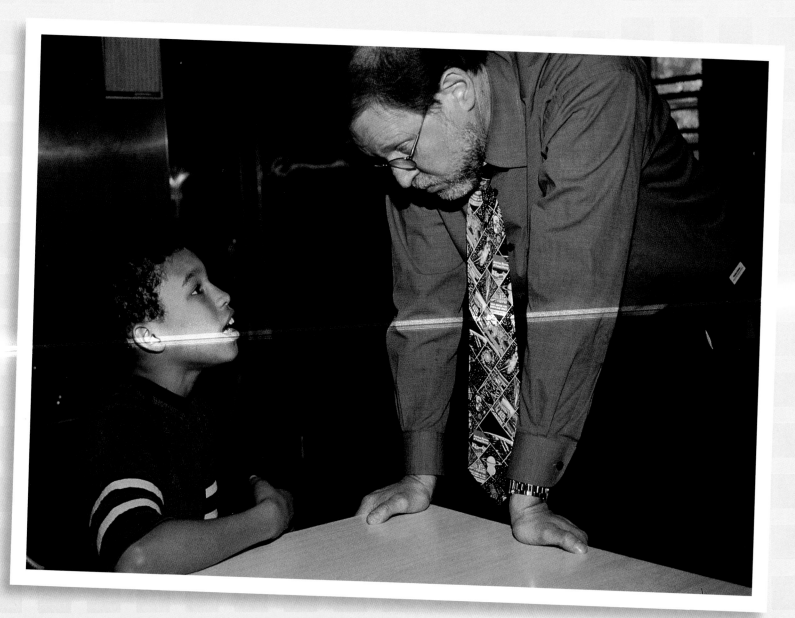

Mr. Plaut in front of his house

Our school is in the city, but Mr. Plaut
lives an hour's ride away. He lives in a pretty
house on a tree-lined street with his wife,
Arleen, and two cats, Tai and T.J.

Mr. Plaut with his wife and Tai, one of his cats

Mr. Plaut with his daughters when they were children

He has two girls, Jen and Melissa, but they are grown and no longer live with him.

When our principal was little, he loved to read and ride ponies.

He still loves to read all kinds of books in a special corner with his stuffed animal collection nearby.

Mr. Plaut was a teacher before he became a principal. But he loves being a principal most of all.

He says the
best part
of being a
principal is
doing so many
different things
to help children
learn.

We know our principal
likes us and we like him!

THAT'S OUR PRINCIPAL!

THINGS TO DO

Would you like to know more about your principal or what it is like to be a principal?

Would you like to do something nice for your principal?

Try one of these activities.

Learn About Your Principal

- Interview your principal to find out all the things a principal does.

- Take some pictures of your principal.

- Make a chart showing all the activities your principal does.

Make A Book

- Make a book about your principal and give it to him or her.

- Your book can tell what your principal does at school and at home. Or it can tell what you like about your principal.

Plan a Principal Day

- Your class can plan a special Principal Day for your principal.

- At the party, you can serve cookies and drinks, sing songs, and give him or her a Principal Book.

About the Author

Ann Morris loves children, and she loves writing books
for children. She has written more than eighty books for
children, including a series of books for The Millbrook
Press about grandmothers and their grandchildren called
What Was It Like, Grandma? For many years Ann Morris
taught school. Eventually, she left teaching to become
an editor with a children's book publishing company.
While she still sometimes teaches workshops and
seminars for teachers, Ann Morris now spends most
of her time writing. She lives in New York City.

About the Photographer-Illustrator

Peter Linenthal is a talented photographer and illustrator.
He studied fine arts at the San Francisco Art Institute.
He is a native of California and teaches at the San Francisco Center
for the Book. Peter Linenthal also loves children
and working on books for children. He did the photographs and
illustrations for Ann Morris's books about grandmothers.